Margaret

I thin[k]

this charming

a city we both enjoy.

Lov

[signature]

A VENETIAN BESTIARY

A VENETIAN
BESTIARY

Jan Morris

faber and faber

First published in the USA in 1982
by Thames and Hudson Inc., New York
First published in 2007
by Faber and Faber Limited
3 Queen Square London WC1N 3AU

Typeset by RefineCatch Ltd, Bungay, Suffolk
Printed in England by Mackays of Chatham, plc

A CIP record for this book
is available from the British Library

ISBN 978-0-571-23305-2

2 4 6 8 10 9 7 5 3 1

CONTENTS

CAST OF CREATURES

Bass · Bear · Bee · Blackbird · Budgerigar
Butterfly · Camel · Canary · Cattle · Cheetah · Cock
Crane · Crocodile · Crow · Curlew · Cuttlefish
Dog · Dolphin · Donkey · Duck · Eagle
Eel · Elephant · Fox · Goose · Gudgeon · Gull
Hawk · Heron · Horse · John Dory · Lark · Lion
Lobster · Minnow · Monkey · Mosquito
Mouse · Mule · Mullet · Nightingale
Octopus · Otter · Owl · Peacock · Pig · Pigeon
Prawn · Rabbit · Rat · Raven · Rhinoceros
Scorpion · Sheep · Shrimp · Snake · Snipe
Stag · Stork · Swallow · Swan · Swift · Swordfish
Tiger · Tortoise · Tuna · Turkey · Whale · Wolf
also Dragons, Griffins, Centaurs, Basilisk
and Winged Lions

In fluctuating temper and varying fortune, in and out of love with the place, I have written rather too much about Venice in the sixty-odd years since the city first bewitched me. This little book, though, I wrote by way of epilogue, and I dedicate it gratefully to all those kind Venetians, human and animal, who have admitted me with such tolerance, over so many years, as a visiting species to their incomparable habitat.

Trefan Morys, 2007

1 THE HABITAT

Tumbling and rushing out of the high Dolomites, streaming across the flatlands of the Veneto, half a dozen rivers of Italy create, on the north-western corner of the Adriatic Sea, the Venetian lagoon. It is an assemblage of estuaries, great and small, thirty-five miles long from one end to the other, seven miles wide at its broadest point. Sheltered from the open sea by intermittent sandy bars, floored with the shale and mud brought down over the centuries by the river waters, littered with islets, it lies in a straggly but symmetrical crescent along the fertile and populous shore, and in satellite pictures looks man-made, as though it has been scooped out of the mainland mechanically, and dammed with the long line of its reefs.

Fifteen centuries ago, when the Roman Empire was falling apart, and Europe was a turmoil of bloodshed and foreboding, this sea-lake became a place of retreat. There were settlements then all along the mainland shore, some of them flourishing cities, with bishops, and rich merchants, and stadiums, and all

3

the appurtenances of provincial life under the Romans. Few people, though, had ever settled within the perimeters of the lagoon. It was a forbidding place all too often, grey and ominous, mud-banks thinly speckled with grass, distant islands lost in mist – a place so desolate that out there in its wastes you could feel a thousand miles from anywhere. In the sunshine it sparkled indeed, and on a bright winter day the spectacle of the snow-capped mountains to the north gave the whole scene a theatrical brilliance: but when the wind blew up with the afternoon tides, chopping the shallow waters, bending the reeds, or when high seas in the Adriatic thundered against the reefs, then the lagoon could be drear and frightening.

It teemed with fish and sea-birds. Half sea, half land, half salt-water, half fresh, it was a strange mixture of living things. If otters and foxes crept down to its mainland creeks, tuna and great eels came in with the tide from the sea. Crabs, prawns, octopuses and a myriad slimy creatures crawled and burrowed among its mudbanks. Duck and geese nested in its marshes. Flowers of the wetlands flourished, bobbed about by butterflies, and on some of the islands pine trees and scrubby vegetation precariously survived. The sounds of the lagoon were wild sounds: the screeching and mewing of sea-birds, the plopping of fish and crustaceans, the whistling of reeds, the hiss and rumble of the open sea beyond the sandbanks.

The only humans to have settled in this fastness were, in one way or another, hunters. Some were professionals: fishermen and duck-hunters who built themselves sea-huts of reed and wood, who roamed the lagoon in flat-bottomed boats and sold their catches in the mainland towns. Some were rich amateurs who liked to entertain their friends at holiday villas in the more accessible reaches. The lagoon was not really remote at all – from its outermost reef you could see, if the weather was right, the towers and houses of the mainland cities: but it was a wilderness all the same, and as things turned out, a refuge.

For by the fifth century the ordered life of the Veneto towns had been hideously disrupted. By then the Empire was collapsing from Britain to the Bosphorus, and sundry rough successors, Huns, Goths, Vandals, were raging across Europe. One by one the prosperous provinces fell, and raids and incursions left the people of the Veneto in a state of perennial terror. Inevitably they took in the end to the lagoon, into whose baffling depths even a Goth would be loath to follow, but precisely how it happened nobody knows. The migration probably began sporadically, people fleeing into the marshes when danger approached, returning to their homes when the barbarians had passed by. Then, perhaps, families or groups of neighbours settled permanently among the waters, gradually building up communities on the less repellent islets. The creation of an independent republic in the heart of the wilderness doubtless took generations to achieve, as separate groups coalesced, as the various settlements combined to elect a common presiding Doge, and as the muddy archipelago called Rivo Alto or Rialto, roughly in the centre of the lagoon, flowered into the city of Venice proper.

This is not, however, as Venetian legend sees it. In the folk-memory Venice was founded at a stroke, and it was a flock of sea-birds that was its guiding spirit. On a March day in the year 421, we are told, the Bishop of Altinum with his entire congregation, carrying their holy objects with them, set off into the lagoon to create a new city – a new Rome, some thought, untainted by blood or barbarism. The Bishop was divinely inspired. Where he saw a flight of birds settle, he had been told in a vision, there he must found the city and so across the marshes prelate and people apprehensively but trustingly ventured, he in his cope and mitre, one supposes, carrying his pastoral staff, they with their bundles and sacks and boxes, cloaked and booted against the raw sea-winds, with their babes-in-arms, and the tools of their trades, and the swaying reliquaries over their heads: and lo! high above them the promised sea-birds wheeled and plummeted, white against the grey sky, beckoning and leading them, circling ever deeper into the lagoon, until at noon on 25 March, with flapping wings and raucous screeches, they settled upon an island in the waste.

The Bishop gave his blessing then, the people prayed, the babies cried, the men began to build their first huts of wattle, thatch and osier, and Venice

6

was founded. The sea-birds dispersed over the waters, and have been loitering there importantly ever since.

* * *

There are times even now, if the weather is right, and the mood perhaps, when the lagoon can still seem almost uninhabited by humankind. Take a boat into its northern extremities, for instance, beyond the ossuary-island of Sant'Ariano, where the bones of the old Venetians lie, and you will find yourself in the original silence of these waters. The towers of Torcello and Burano are lost among the reeds, the Iesolo hotels are no more than bright blurs on the seaward horizon, and Venice itself is out of sight to the south. The only living things about you are the things that were always there: the sea-birds, the little brown crabs, the butterflies, the fish who splash and gasp sometimes among the rushes. It is as though the Bishop had never followed those gulls into the wilderness after all.

This is the countryside of Venice: and though the lagoon is criss-crossed now by navigation channels, and spindled with marker-posts, and traversed by great tankers on their way to the mainland refineries, and furrowed by a thousand motor-boats, and water-buses, and cruise ships, still these deserted corners are not hard to find, and they mean that the great city itself is never far from the simplicities and subtleties of nature. The very wateriness of the lagoon, of the city indeed, where the streets are canals, and the buses are boats, gives Venice a powerfully organic feel: with its towers and palaces jammed there upon their mud-banks, it often seems less like a human artifact than some crusted pile of water-deposits, built up age after age by the rise and fall of the tides. Visitors to Venice pine sometimes for the green of meadows and parklands, but the lagoon itself has always been the true estate of Venice, the fishermen its farmers, the mullet, the prawns, the gulls its natural livestock.

It is true that from the mainland shore these days a haze of chemicals drifts over the lagoon: if you can still sometimes see those snow-ridges, more often it is only the refineries and shipyards of Mestre, the aircraft of Marco Polo airport or the scurrying cars of the Trieste autostrada, that glint in the sun across the waters. Before long, I dare say, the loneliest islets will be developed for the tourists, and the line of the sea-reefs will be one uninterrupted promenade of hotels and casinos. Nevertheless even now the Venetian citizen has only to board his evening *vaporetto* for the Lido, and sail away for his short voyage home across the Bacino di San Marco, the Basin of St Mark, to feel himself on the edge of wild waters, as the islands stand away, one by one in the evening haze, towards the unfrequented reaches of the lagoon. It is as though your Parisian commuter, say, or your New Yorker, were to take his evening bus home along the rim of a bleak moorland, where curlews cried, or badgers lolloped in the headlights. Hints of desolation creep into the very courtyards of Venice, blown by the sea-winds, carried on the fog.

As a result, through much of their history the Venetians themselves were seen by more prosaic peoples as less, or more, than ordinarily human. They were like sea-birds themselves, thought the sixth-century Byzantine Cassiodorus, their homes 'dispersed . . . across the surface of the waters'. They were like fish, thought the fifteenth-century Pope Pius II, 'and as among brute beasts aquatic creatures have the least intelligence, so among human beings the Venetians are the least just and the least capable of humanity . . .' The strangeness of their circumstances, the improbable power they established in their lagoon, made them seem of some other species, on another plane of the divine creation.

And conversely perhaps, it gave them a special affinity with the natural order of things. They lived far closer to their own element, the water, than other city-people did to theirs, the land; and so over generations, for all their urbane sophistication, they retained a profound feeling for the birds, the fishes and the beasts. It was not I think any mystic thrall: it was rather an honest and affectionate familiarity, a kind of comradeship, which brought the animal creation robustly into their life, art and symbolism. Throughout the history of Venice, through the thousand years of its republican independence, its conquest by Napoleon, its incorporation into Italy and its ambivalent condition today, part museum, part conference centre, part holiday camp – throughout it all the city has cherished, celebrated and sometimes exalted its animals. Those creatures of the lagoon, of the air, the marsh and the salt-water, were reinforced soon by beasts of a wider experience: fish and fowl, crustacea and lepidoptera, mammals and reptiles and chimerae of several persuasions were absorbed into the public sensibility, and created a civic bestiary, in the mind and in the flesh, that was unlike any other.

* * *

So when you pole your boat out of those northern shallows, and sail back past the spooky bone-island, past the leaning tower of Burano, past Murano's grubby glass-works, into the canals of the great city itself, you will be entering a mighty menagerie of fact and fantasy – beasts tender and ferocious, historical and imaginary, repulsive and enchanting – furred, feathered, scaled, skinned and occasionally all four at once – beasts in paint and in stonework, beasts of bronze and beasts of marble, beasts symbolic, beasts heraldic, haughty beasts of political import, sweet beasts born of lyric fancy – beasts dead on market stalls or dinner plates, beasts in the memory or the metaphor, beasts in the desire, and above all beasts alive and breathing still, soaring dream-like above your head, yapping through wicker muzzles among the legs of the Piazza tourists, scuttling here and there among the barnacles, or complacently washing their whiskers after meals of left-over spaghetti in the shadowy undersides of bridges.

2 FLIGHT OF BIRDS

The fancy of the Venetians was captured first by the birds, free as they were to move between three of the four elements (the phoenix mastered the fourth too, of course, and accordingly gave his name to the Venetian opera house, La Fenice). Birds figured prominently in the early Venetian myths: not only did they guide those first settlers to their destination, but more than once they told the Venetians where best to build their island churches – 'where a number of birds shall gather together', or 'where twelve cranes shall be in company'. No doubt the people identified themselves with the sea-birds of the lagoon, as Cassiodorus identified them, making their own nests among its reeds and mud-banks, and roaming with more ease than most of humanity between land, sea and air.

It was a joyous freedom that the Venetian artists bestowed in particular upon the birds, when they came to portray the Creation. There is a thirteenth-century mosaic in the Basilica San Marco, for instance, in which a sea already over-populated with fish is flown over by a wonderfully dashing and ebullient variety of birds – a couple of gulls naturally, a heron, a snipe perhaps (the lagoon is its southernmost habitat), a black crow, what looks like an owl, all throwing themselves about the golden sky, wings akimbo so to speak, in a fierce ecstasy of emancipation. Birds distinctly set the pace of the Fifth Day, too, in Tintoretto's version of the event, painted in the 1550s. The animals are rambling here and there, on the overcast shore of the world, the tiger taking a drink, the tortoise dozing, the stag grazing a hillside: but lustily into the morning fly the birds in reproductive pairs, geese and duck and curlew, white swans far behind, streaming so exuberantly across the sky that their Creator has exerted his divine prerogatives in response, and radiant with his own glory takes to flight himself.

They are mostly water-birds, as you might expect. Birds of many kinds frequent the landward reaches of the lagoon, and caged birds in their thousands, blackbirds, nightingales and larks until recently, now only budgerigars and canaries, have always rustled and twittered in the alleys of the city – caged singing-birds used to play an official part in the installation of a new Doge. By the nature of things, though, the gulls and the wild duck are the most truly Venetian birds. Night and day the white herring-gulls flock around the waterfronts, perched on the tops of water-stakes, following the ships through the Bacino di San Marco, scavenging around the fish market as dawn breaks over Venice. Not so long ago one even saw them on sale in the markets themselves, tied together head-down in ignominious bundles, and tasting when well-boiled, they used to say, palatable but fishy.

The duck is fair game for the sportsman still, and still in the small hours, in the remoter parts of the lagoon, you may hear the sudden thunder of the hunter's gun as he lies in his boat among the reeds – a special kind of boat, too, called the *s'ciopon*, which carries its great gun at the prow as an old galleasse carried its cannon. It was always so. One of the hoarier Venetian traditions was the Doge's enthronement gift, to each member of the Grand Council, of five wild duck apiece, carefully balanced as to fat or thin; by the early sixteenth century, when the Council had been greatly enlarged, a new Doge had to supply nearly nine thousand birds, so the tribute was commuted into the presentation of a specially minted medal (and thus the Venetian duck gave a name to one of the great coins of the Republic, the *osella* – though not, as frivolous Englishmen have suggested, to the *ducat*).

Many of those Ducal birds were snared, but many more were shot with bows and arrows, as the Romans of the Veneto had shot them long before, and the Venetians continued to hunt their duck by archery, using terracotta bullets, down to the eighteenth century. Two painters, Vittore Carpaccio in the sixteenth century, Pietro Longhi in the eighteenth, have left us farcical representations of such outings. In the earlier scene seven boats are in the hunt, oarsmen and bowmen alike stretched taut with concentration, but the birds, half of which seem to be cormorants, are altogether unmoved by the threat: some sit casually on posts, two or three swim about with only their heads protruding from the water, one has actually settled upon one of the boats, and most of the others are streaming away into a cloudy sky in contemptuously disciplined formation. In Longhi's picture the birds seem rather less safe. This is an altogether statelier shoot, the solitary huntsman being a grand signor armed with a long-bow and attended by four respectful servants, and his mood is distinctly dignified – the huntsman is in the act of drawing his bow, the men stand frozen at their oars, in the middle distance a solitary water-fowl paddles urgently towards the horizon, and all around the islanded lagoon lies in a sort of watchful hush. It seems to have been a decorous entertainment, sportsman, servants, duck, lagoon itself collaborating: it was the traditional hunt of the Venetian gentleman, the tally-ho of the lagoon.

Just occasionally you may see a swan over Venice, winging a lordly way southward to the Ravenna marshes, or in search of a nesting-place in the Brenta water-meadows. It is a thousand years, I dare say, since one of these noble birds really alighted in Venice itself, but in one of the earliest of all known paintings of the city, an imaginative miniature from the fourteenth- or fifteenth-century manuscript called *The Book of Marco Polo*, a swan-flotilla gracefully ornaments the scene. The city itself is dazzling with colour in this cheerful portrayal, its towers topped with blue and gold, its citizens flamboyantly robed, its lagoon neatly rippled, its ships flying pennants every one, and in the heart of the scene, almost as large as the ships themselves, four brilliantly white swans look as though they own the place. One faces east, one faces west, and two are upturned in the water, only their feathered rumps in sight.

* * *

If water-birds were the original familiars of Venice, swifts and swallows have always been its exhilarating visitants. Out of the south they come each summer, like messengers, bringing with them the promise of warmth and revived prosperity, and catching the hearts of watchers on the way – as Browning wrote,

> There goes a swallow to Venice – the stout sea-farer!
> Seeing those birds fly makes one wish for wings.

They arrive in the middle of June, and in earlier times they were welcomed not only for their dancing vivacity, but also for their appetites. Almost until our own days a perennial scourge of Venice was the mosquito, *anopheles maculipennis*: in the Middle Ages this insect is said to have depopulated several of the lagoon islands, and in the nineteenth century it was a principal preoccupation of tourists. John Murray's *Handbook to Northern Italy* advised them not only to close all their windows tightly at sunset, but actually to *sew up the curtains*; his rival Baedeker suggested hanging a rag soaked in petroleum at the head of the bed, or burning a particular kind of pastille (though this was 'accompanied', as he had to admit, 'by a scarcely agreeable odour').

Come June, though, came the blessed swallows, and rag, pastille, needle and thread could be put away, windows cautiously opened to the evening air: for swooping debonairly about the rooftops, in no time at all they had *anopheles maculipennis* more or less under control. Today the mosquitoes have nearly all vanished anyway, and the swifts and swallows, denied perhaps their proper diet, are not so apparent either: but still those birds speak of Venice, to susceptible spectators far away, and as they streak away with their excited jerks and chatters towards the sunshine make one wish for wings.

* * *

In Tintoretto's *Creation of the Animals* there are a couple of birds that look very like pigeons; in Carpaccio's *Departure of St Ursula* a sort of pigeon, dominating the foreground of the picture, intently examines the artist's signature. It is proper that they should be immortalized thus in Venetian art, for if there is one living creature that the world associates instinctively with Venice, it is the common grey pigeon, which infests in almost verminous profusion the Piazza San Marco, the great central square of the city, gobbling and strutting about the pavements, swarming over the persons of indulgent visitors, gliding inconsiderately here and there or clinging to pediments and window-sills high above, where their ruffled shapes lurk in every crevice like the souls of the grey dead in limbo.

The pigeon is, if not actually sacred, at least highly respected in Venice. You will never be offered him roasted in a Venetian restaurant. On the contrary, sometimes invalid pigeons, having lost a leg perhaps in a more than unusually unseemly scramble for peanuts, become known individually to the waiters at the Piazza cafés, and are thereafter privileged for life, allowed to preen themselves on unoccupied tables, and fed wonderfully sustaining morsels of toasted sandwich. Pigeons can get away with almost anything in Venice, and sometimes you will see one, all puffed up with pride, swaggering into the narthex of the Basilica San Marco itself.

It is said that the apotheosis of the Venetian pigeon occurred in 1204, when the Doge Enrico Dandolo, having presided over the capture of Constantinople by the Fourth Crusade, sent the good news home by carrier bird – 900 miles it must have flown, across the breadth of the Balkans. Another theory is that the pigeons' immunity was established by an old Palm Sunday tradition, in which flights of doves were released into the sky in the Piazza. Whatever the cause, the bird became a kind of national mascot, and dove-bowls of Istrian stone were scooped into the courtyard of the Doge's Palace itself, as if in diplomatic recognition. It was in Venice that *columba livia* first became thoroughly urbanized: even in the twentieth century, when foreign municipalities have wanted to set up pigeon-stock of their own, they have sometimes come to Venice for a pair of the real things.

For many years the Piazza pigeons were fed at the city's expense, but in the 1950s an insurance company undertook their maintenance as an advertising device, and the daily ritual became one of the more curious of Venetian events. A misty winter morning was the best time to see it, when the square was still empty of people, the top of the Campanile San Marco was lost in vapour, and the birds were huddled silent in their crannies all around. Just before nine o'clock an official appeared with two big bins of maize, but when the first clocks struck the hour across the foggy city, not a soul took any notice: the man stood impassive, the birds stirred not a pinion. A long moment passed: and then, when the great bell of the Campanile itself immensely sounded, suddenly the eerie cameo burst into movement. The man scurried across the square emptying his bins behind him; the horde of grey pigeons, scratching, pushing, bobbing, swooping like bats out of their roosts, fell maniacally upon their victuals.

Only for a second or two did the insurance company get its money's worth: for there was just time to see, before the doves destroyed the pattern, that the maize had been poured on the ground in the

shape of two huge letters – A.G., for Assicurazioni
Generali.

* * *

By and large birds figured only as extras in Venetian
painting. We see a hawk attacking a crane in Carpaccio
once, a stork confronting a serpent in Giovanni Bellini,
and Tintoretto paints a delightful pair of ducks snuf-
fling water-insects in a pond as the Israelites gather
their manna in the desert. Here and there appear the
caged birds so beloved of the Venetians, and the mischievous Pietro Longhi balances an infant popinjay on
horseback, in his picture *The Horseback Ride*, with a real
live turkey-cock in the foreground.

Birds more frequently achieve star status, though,
in the sculptures and mosaics of the city. Three of the
column capitals of the Doge's Palace are devoted to
them – birds flying and roosting and preening themselves, birds clawed and webbed, a bird eating a fish,
a bird fighting a snake, not to speak of the game-bird
who is being swallowed by Gluttony, or the cock who
has been mangled by a wolf. Symbolic birds of many
kinds are carved on the city's lesser buildings, too:
eagles have plump pineapple bodies, the elegant peacock, Byzantine symbol of the Resurrection, parades
in bas-relief or archivolt, and many a less identifiable
bird leaps allegorically at the throat of an animal, or
alternatively shares responsibility with him for the
support of a pillar.

From them all, let us choose three to stand representative. A comical bird first: in the public gardens at the eastern end of the Riva degli Schiavoni a nineteenth-century Minerva sits sideways upon a lion, and on her head reposes the funniest and most endearing little owl imaginable – rotund, wide-eyed, and gifted by some jolly whim of the sculptor's mind with unmistakable *knees*. Next a bizarre but useful bird: at the Rialto end of the Mercerie, the chief shopping street of Venice, affixed high upon a wall there stands a greenish metal crane, an Art Nouveau version of the ancient bird of vigilance, with swooping neck and glaring eyes – a spiky metallic creature, but gratefully recognized by every tourist, for without his elongated neck to point the way, leering down the years over the passing throng, hardly a visitor in a thousand could ever find the right alley-way back to the hotel.

And thirdly, a faithless bird, a bird without a conscience. The raven is hardly a Venetian familiar – you will never hear his guttural croak on these salt winds – but he it was whom Noah first released from the Ark to test the state of the Flood, and I dare say the old Venetians, when they rehearsed the tale, imagined him winging his way across the waters of their own lagoon. When it came to portraying the event in the mosaics of the Basilica, the anonymous thirteenth-century artist put a black humour into the image. Noah, having released the bird, leans out of the Ark hopefully awaiting his return, holding the dove in reserve, but the raven has discovered something not very pleasant to eat among the floating carnage of the deluge; and there he flutters at the water's surface, very sharp, very bright, very predatory, birdness itself exemplified in his sharp outline against the rippled water, so intent upon his grisly pleasures that he has forgotten his mission altogether.

3 SCHOOL OF SEA-CREATURES

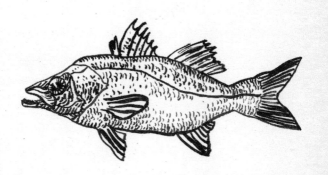

Many a sea-creature, as in the beginnings of time, has squirmed and squelched out of the shallows to join the Venetian bestiary. The Adriatic Sea is wonderfully rich in marine organisms, the lagoon has an ecology of its own, and between them at the beginning of this century they were said to nurture 150 varieties of fish. It is not surprising that the imagination, the art and not least the cuisine of Venice has always been fishily or amphibianally enriched. Venice is built upon piles among the mud, and through its very foundations the fish flicker, the shrimps jump and the big eels curl themselves.

Each day some of them are caught, while many more are brought in from the Adriatic fishing ports, and they are displayed in slimy proliferation at the fish market beside the Rialto bridge, on the marble slabs of its central hall, or on stalls beside the waterfront on the Grand Canal. The market smells aggressively aquatic, its floors are slippery with discarded fins or decapitations, its air is loud with the crunched axeing of tuna-steaks or the clatter of bucketed crabs, and all around are strange shapes and matters of the underwater – not simply shining flanks and scaled strips, but tubes, and tentacles, and bulbous shells, and writhing string-like things, and goggle-eyes, and blodges of jelly, and claws still groping, and legs still hopping, and big lugubrious prawns.

Fish are fundamental to the Venetian style, if only because for centuries the Venetians mostly ate nothing else. They had one great wealth, Cassiodorus said, 'the fish which suffices for them all', and even eighty years ago almost all those 150 species were thought fit for the table. Fishing was the *raison d'être* of the very first watery settlements, and fishermen figure largely in the Venetian myths and annals. Until the Second World War the painted sails of the *bragozzi*, the deep-sea fishing vessels of the Venetians, were still a familiar sight within the reefs: and even in our polluted times, like elegant insects on the surface of the water, the fishermen of the lagoon, in their slender black *sandoli*, can be seen far in the wilderness casting their nets among the shallows, prodding the staked mussel beds, or inspecting the fish farms of the south.

When that disagreeable old Pope likened the Venetians themselves to fish, perhaps he was half-right: after so many generations of intimate contact with the fishes, after so many centuries of their absorption, surely by very osmosis the Venetians have become partly piscine themselves. Surely there is more than mere gourmandism, but actually empathy to the care with which your Venetian burgher, dining out at his favourite restaurant, selects mullet, brill, bass or John Dory from the glistening pile of fish-corpses laid out in green sea-fronds by the door. Tourists may find, slumped uncompromisingly before them, the Venetian inescapable called *fritto misto*, a few bits of fish, a cuttlefish or two, heavily disguised in fried bread-crumbs: the native eats his fish on more respectful terms, and has his pot-pourri of the sea steamed in a paper bag, or sympathetically melted into soup, or synthesized with rice in the elegiac dish called *risotto nero*, in which all is thickened and blackened by the ink of the squid . . .

And just as the fish is ubiquitous in the Venetian diet, so it is pickled in the Venetian sensibility. The city never tires of its fishiness. At the turn of the twentieth century a well-known local hawker used to tow a dolphin up and down the Grand Canal, while the enthusiastic citizenry threw coins from the windows above, and today too all along the quaysides you may see the Venetians trying to re-establish their connections with the deep. Some are silent and meditative over their rods, some are gregariously talkative – some are disreputable small boys, some church-going matrons – but even at the present stage of life among the lagoons, when at last a fish is caught, and is whipped wriggling out of the water, a sense of wonder seems to seize the bystanders, and they hasten to the fisherman's box to see the creature lying there, and stare at it silently over each other's shoulders, while the proud angler looks almost artistically self-satisfied – as though he has not simply hooked the creature for his supper, but actually created it.

*   *   *

A sense of wonder also informs the work of Venetian artists in a more orthodox kind, when they represent the sea-creatures. If those birds of Tintoretto's *Creation* flew into the sunrise in a fine libertarian flourish, the fishes down below swam off in an amazing motion, urgently half out of the water, some of them grinning foolishly: and a strange collection of creatures they are, for while in the foreground swims an unmistakable red mullet, further away there flounder out to sea a wild variety of demi-dolphins, neo-swordfish and pseudo-lobsters.

Fish swim weirdly, green and long-snouted, through several of Venice's Byzantine mosaics. A disturbing panel of them, as crowded and queer as a coral reef, appears in the Creation scene in one of the cupolas of the Basilica – there is the great whale, there are the gudgeon and the minnows, fine fat lobsters crawl about, and mightily amongst them moves the sea-monster, with crescent claws and rapacious teeth. Crab and swordfish lurk in the Jordan, in the Basilica's fourteenth-century version of Christ's baptism, and the attentions of man-eating fish are amongst the torments promised the wicked in the Universal Judgment mosaic in the island cathedral of Torcello. The Gothic ornamenters of the city also liked their marine life: the tuna-fish, an unexpected favourite of mediaeval sculpture, repeatedly appears, while the crab and the dolphin are both immortalized upon the Doge's Palace capitals – the crab in a basket, poor thing, the dolphin toothily at sea with Arion playing the violin on his back.

Sometimes they are amphibiously mutated versions of themselves. Fish tails are grafted on to griffins, dolphins' snouts have lions' rumps, and this may be because the Venetians, the most amphibious of human beings, preferred their sea-creatures bi-elemental too. Tom Coryat, a seventeenth-century English visitor to Venice, reported that 'amongst many other strange fishes that I have observed in their market-places, I have seene many Torteises', and for several centuries another incongruous amphibian provided the Venetian Republic with one of its reigning symbols.

The original patron saint of Venice was St Theodore, and the first church in Venice proper, somewhere near the site of the present Basilica, was dedicated to him. His identity is questionable. Was he the military martyr St Theodore of Heraclea, or the warrior-saint Theodore Tiro? Was he the Abbot Theodore the Sanctified, or the Bishop St Theodore of Sykeon, or the monk St Theodore the Studite? Or was he, as Coryat was told, no more than a former Venetian commander-in-chief, locally canonized for his belligerence? Whoever he was, a statue was raised in his honour on top of a magnificent marble pillar in the Piazzetta San Marco, around the corner from the Basilica and immediately outside the Doge's Palace.

At his feet, for reasons we do not know, there lies a lumpish crocodile. Perhaps he was a pet. Perhaps he is meant to be a dragon. He squats there anyway, docile below that stalwart saint – himself reconstructed, incidentally, in 1888 – and for eight hundred years he has been an eminence among the Venetian beasts. In that very first city view, the one with the swans, he is already vaguely to be discerned upon his column (though the saint has sprouted wings there, and seems to be thrashing the beast). He is not a very lovely animal, to be honest, but his presence is part of the Venetian order, part of the family feeling, and it is pleasant to fancy that perhaps he was not hoisted up there at all, but crawled out of the sea one evening long ago, and labouring across the Piazzetta, inching himself scratchily claw by claw up the pillar, deposited himself voluntarily, and for ever more, beside his master's feet.

4 PACK OF DOGS

Deep in the water with its cargo of vegetables, or furniture, or beer-bottles, a stout Venetian barge comes chugging down the Grand Canal, puffing exhaust fumes from its little black funnel. At its stern sits a characteristic specimen of *homo Venetiaticus*, clad in blue overalls, steering the boat with one arm negligently over the tiller, tapping his feet very likely to the music of his transistor radio, and looking as though, if the need arose, he would take his boat there and then to Singapore.

At the prow stands a no less typical example of the Venetian citizenry: for there facing the wind, his tail high, his teeth shining, his tongue out, steady as a rock upon the deck, a fine proletarian dog rides the great highway in glory. He is all life there, all vigour. Sometimes he turns impulsively on his heels and trots back to the stern for a pat on the head: but always he returns to his watchpost again, and so we see him ruffled and quivering with responsibility as the barge takes a sudden swing to port, and passing beneath the dappled arch of a bridge, disappears from view.

Who can doubt that when those first columns of refugees timorously embarked into the reeds, the first of the Venetian dogs went with them? They were probably just watchdogs first, but they have long since become the most beloved animals in Venetian life, and among the most honoured in Venetian art. They are not all Gothic barge dogs. On the contrary, they are often pampered and patrician dogs, splendid dogs in set-piece paintings, lap-dogs, merry little terriers, showy dogs for exhibitionist décors, dogs to be confided in by jewelled dowagers, or romped with by children in the backgrounds of ceremonies. In Victorian times they often used to be shaved; today they are likely to be lovingly clipped, brightly collared and sometimes ribboned.

They are never savage dogs. They snarl only in fun, or for effect, and in the streets as in the pictures seem almost unnaturally serene of temperament. The Venetian dog is a favoured beast, after all. No car is going to run him down. No sadist is going to beat him. All he must do in life is look friendly, sit neat, dignify the prows of boats or lie voluptuously on the counterpanes of odalisques. In our own times the best-known animal in Venetian life has undoubtedly been the indolent old retriever who used to laze all day long around the *traghetto* ferry-station beside the Gritti Palace Hotel, the familiar of every visitor, sprawling there on the flagstones while the gondoliers chatted in the sun behind him, and heavily thumping his great tail, slightly stirring his idle old face, when somebody stooped to greet him.

* * *

The world's favourite canine Venetian is certainly the Carpaccio dog. Vittore Carpaccio portrayed this entrancing creature often, in various breeds, guises and conditions, but his archetype, so to speak, appeared in a picture which the artist painted for the Confraternity of Slavs in Venice, one of a series which still ornament the walls of their headquarters, the Scuola San Giorgio degli Schiavoni. The picture shows a saintly scholar, probably St Augustine, sitting at his study desk. He is surrounded by the tools of his craft, books open all over the place, an armillary sphere hanging from the ceiling, a pen in his hand, and he is looking out of his window into the sunshine – hearing a voice from Heaven, if he *is* Augustine. As he stares out there, from the floor below his terrier stares at him. This adorable little animal sits there bright-eyed, black-nosed and cock-eared, covered all over with tangled curls, alert and attentive to every flicker of his master's mood: and finding his way into a thousand albums, a million picture postcards, for generations of admirers the dog has stolen the scene from the saint.

Elsewhere the Carpaccio dog can be very different. He sits smooth-haired, for instance, and rather less vivacious, beside the saint's four-poster in *The Dream*

of St Ursula. He lounges in a jewelled collar, carefully
tousled one feels, in a nobleman's gondola in *The
Miracle of the True Cross at the Rialto*. Collared again,
and with an unsightly mole on his right cheek, he sits
on his haunches with his front paws in the hand of a
bored, bored lady in the picture called *Two Cour-
tesans*: behind him a rather less endearing cousin,
teeth bared in play, is worrying the lady's stick, but
our little friend is all docile commiseration – never
mind, he seems to be telling his mistress, *I'm* here,
and as he does so he turns his head to look at the
painter himself, and his eternal audience, full and
confiding in the eye. The Carpaccio dog is ever faith-
ful, ever watchful: it is no coincidence that in several
pictures the artist stations him as sentinel over his
own signature (though it is true that a lizard does the
job once).

He is alive and thriving to this day, too, and you
can hardly escape him as you walk about the city. He
often takes the form nowadays of a lickety-spit variety of Tibetan terrier, like an animated small ball of
wool, to be seen tumbling about the Riva degli Schiavoni with a friend or two, larking with the children
on their way home from school, or snoozing flat out
among the souvenir stalls. His origins seem confused,
his pedigree is doubtful, but even when he is all
bundled up in his muzzle, as the law somewhat
ineffectually decrees, he remains as lovable and
reliable as ever he was, when he sat so attentively
upon that study floor, keeping an eye on the sage.

* * *

The kind-hearted Venetians never tire of their dogs, whether they be these rapscallion terriers or the mighty cross-breeds of the vegetable barges, and there was scarcely another artist, through the centuries of Venetian painting, who did not include dogs somewhere among his compositions.

Sometimes they are there for relief, in one kind or another. A dwarf and a dog together, for example, temper the overwhelming pomp of Giambattista Tiepolo's *Banquet of Anthony and Cleopatra*, painted in fresco in the 1740s in the hall of the Palazza Labia, while Giorgione, painting three centuries before, has a sleepy hound taking absolutely no notice at all of the Judgment of Paris. Even in devout religious pictures, dogs are often there to give an earthier dimension to the scene: a bounding impatient dog chivvies Tobias and his Angel in a painting by one of the eighteenth-century Guardi family in the church of Angelo Raffaele; a wispy lapdog attends the virgin in Lorenzo Lotto's seventeenth-century Annunciation; a dog looks on incuriously while Tintoretto's Christ washes his disciples' feet; and the fifteenth-century master Giambattista Cima, in one of his Nativities, places a small dog in the foreground, looking interestedly as it were off-stage, as though to remind us that even at the holiest of moments everyday things are happening out of sight – a cat crossing a roof perhaps, a bone thrown out by a butcher.

At other times dogs are included in a spirit of satire or caprice, or just for fun. In many of Pietro Longhi's mischievous family portraits a dog looks comically like his owners – pug to dowager, poodle to belle; in his picture *The Perfume-Seller*, showing an old woman selling scents in the street, two dogs at the edge of the tableau are sniffing each other appreciatively, while in *The Little Concert* nobody pays any attention to the quartet, stringing away there in the centre of the composition, except a rapt little white dog on a table. Giandomenico Tiepolo, in a painting called *The Walk*, shows a patrician family *en promenade* accompanied by a greyhound so exactly their parody, so identically blasé of manner, languid of gait, stooped and aloof of figure, that one almost expects him to be joining in their conversation. Look nearly anywhere in the view-pictures of Canaletto or Francesco Guardi, the supreme delineators of eighteenth-century Venice, and you will see dogs; and in Guardi's pictures especially they seem to be entirely their own masters, wandering the streets in perfect liberty, or meeting their friends for a gossip precisely like the humans up above.

* * *

But sometimes there feels to be some deeper meaning to the presence of a dog in a Venetian painting, some arcane or allegorical allusion. Kenneth Clark observed that in several of Titian's sixteenth-century portraits the human subject is looking somewhere else, and only his attendant dog looks directly into the eye of the artist – 'establishing a sort of secret contact'. Elsewhere Titian's dogs seem intended to point a moral contrast – a solid, plain-featured gun-dog, for instance, at the feet of a gaudy aristocrat, or the two great hunting-dogs which, in his *Venus and Adonis* at the Prado, seem intent on snatching their master away from emasculating entanglements. Dogs add intriguing nuances to Titian's several nudes too: in the *Venus of Urbino* it is a soft little dog like a King Charles spaniel, curled up snug and sleepy at the lady's feet; in the *Danaë* at the Prado it is a silky dachshund, over whose sleeping head her hand sensuously plays; in the *Venus with an Organist*, while a black boy provides the music, and a lascivious cupid stimulates the eroticism, it is a fluffy white terrier, teeth bared at the bottom right of the picture, who suggests an element of danger.

More particularly still, critics profess to detect enigmatic symbolisms in the dogs of Paolo Veronese, the supreme Venetian dog-master, the whipper-in of all this pack, whose sumptuous palace scenes, pagan in spirit but Christian in pretension, gorgeously reflect the style of sixteenth-century Venice. Most of these huge canvases and frescos include dogs, and often they do seem to have been placed there to point philosophical, moral, religious or perhaps political meanings: so pointedly indeed did Veronese position a big retriever in the foreground of the *Last Supper* he painted for monastic clients in 1573 that the Inquisition itself ordered him to replace it by a figure of Mary Magdalene (he declined, and instead just renamed the picture *The Feast at the House of Levi*).

But I don't believe it. I think Veronese's dogs are there, front-stage or in the wings, simply because he loved them so. They are dogs of love, the supreme exemplars of an old Venetian addiction, and their prominence in his pictures is evidence only of his mastery of their forms – as Ruskin said of his dog-portraits, 'the essence of dog is there, the entire, magnificent, generic animal type, muscular and living'. They are not super-dogs, or artistic similes. They behave as all dogs do. Their back-ends disappear beneath tables, children fondle them behind the scenes at banquets, they are suddenly awakened from sleep, or they are caught in that unmistakable dog-posture, head down, haunches twisted, which means that they are just about to scratch themselves.

5 PRIDE OF CATS

Here's a curiosity. In Carpaccio's original sketch for that picture in the saint's study, all is much the same as it would be in the final painted version. The holy man sits in just the same attitude, the books are similarly scattered, the sphere hangs from the rafters. There is, however, one important variation, for it turns out that the little white dog began life, in embryo as it were, not as a dog at all, but as a scrunchy and distinctly unconvincing *cat*. Evidently recognizing its shortcomings, Carpaccio switched species, and never so far as I know attempted a domestic cat again.

This is odd, for his pictures are rich in creatures of every kind, but by no means unique. If every great Venetian artist could paint a superlative dog, hardly one of them could paint an adequate cat. Veronese once painted an excellent cat's head, no more, Lorenzo Lotto has one fine black prowler in a background, and Jacopo Bassano, in the sixteenth century, caught a pair of country cats admirably among the multitudinous creatures of his *Animals*

Entering the Ark. Otherwise the cats are mostly hope-less. Lotto gives us a cat like a rat, Tintoretto a cat like a hyena, Giovanni Bellini a cat like a monkey, and Pietro Longhi a cat curled up under a table like a nightmare raccoon.

Perhaps the cat was too impatient a sitter, or seemed to the Venetian mind, so impressed by grandeur and fidelity, a little flibbertigibbet for art. It was certainly not unfamiliarity that inhibited the artists, or even lack of affection, for Venice has always been one of the great cat-cities of the world: before the Second World War there were said to be 40,000 cats in the city, one for every four humans, and there are still few places in Europe where the cat is more indulgently regarded, or more enviably free of spirit. There is even a street named for the cats of Venice – well, for half of them, because grammatically speaking Salizzada delle Gatte is dedicated only to the females.

* * *

For one thing the cat has always been an essential scavenger in a city that depends on the tides for its hygiene, and has periodically been decimated by rat-borne plagues. It was Shylock the Venetian who declared the cat to be 'both necessary and harmless', and when from time to time the municipality has tried to reduce the teeming feline population, the citizenry has always been up in arms in protest. Your Venetian cats are not like others. Sometimes of course they live

48

in the bosoms of families, and are fed on canned horse-meat, and prettied up with bows; but far more often they survive half-wild, in feral gangs or covens of cats, and not infrequently some cherished household pet, observing the lives of such lucky ruffians from the kitchen window, will abandon the comforts of basket and fireside rug, and take to the streets himself.

Cats, alas, are diminishing in Venice, but they are familiars of the city still. You come across them sitting bolt upright in gardens, scattered among the grass like so many statuettes. You find them sprawling in purring groups in the sunshine, or skulking in door-ways, or peering out at you from holes in old walls. They slink from shadow to shadow before your tread, they leap like lightning over garden walls, they scrabble among the market offal, they help them-selves adeptly to water from drinking-pipes, they are curled up fast asleep in the shade of upturned gondo-las, or on ancient palace steps. You discover their communal lairs unexpectedly. Not an animal is in sight as you cross a wooden bridge, say, or pass a clump of bushes in the public gardens; but there in the shadow you catch a glimpse of cats as you pass, an impression of cats, huddled conspiratorially under the bridge-boards, crouched among the leaves.

Often there are tell-tale scraps of old brown paper around, for the cats of Venice, however scrawny or unapproachable, are never without their benefactors. Innumerable kind ladies see that their local vagabond tribes are fed, with pungent meat-balls, fish-heads, or the viscous remains of the day's pasta. One seldom sees a really undernourished cat in Venice – and when the spring comes indeed, and the cats plump themselves out with the extra pickings of the tourist industry, then the females among them one and all seem to swell maternally too, and another generation of young toughs scrabbles out of the stonework into the city.

*　*　*

There have been a few celebrity-cats in Venetian history. For instance there was the cat who was the great love of the seventeenth-century Doge Francesco Morosini, conqueror of the Peloponnese – his only love, it has been said, except that of his country's glory. Morosini (who habitually dressed himself, by the way, entirely in red from top to toe) took the animal on all his campaigns, on the poop of his galley at sea, in his command tent on land, and when the cat died the old hero kept her skeleton like a holy relic.

Or there was Nini the Frari cat. This genial animal lived, in the second half of the nineteenth century, in a café near the Frari church and the Venetian Archives, and became well-known to visitors to either of those buildings – so well-known indeed that in later years people made pilgrimages to the district just to see *him*. He was not a very special cat in himself – just a jolly white domestic tom – but around him there grew a dead-pan cult, rather like the mock-serious fraternity that has grown up around the fictions of Sherlock Holmes and Bertie Wooster. Nini's fame was skilfully exploited by his owner the café proprietor, and the cat had his own visitor's book, dutifully signed by swells of every kind.

A Pope, a Czar of Russia, an Emperor of Ethiopia all called on Nini. So did Metternich, and Verdi scribbled in the cat's book a few notes of Act III of *La Traviata* (magnanimously perhaps, for the opera's first performance, at the nearby Fenice in 1853, had been a humiliating fiasco). When the cat died writers, artists and poets hastened to offer obituary tributes. 'A rare gem', said one, 'most honest of creatures'. 'A gentleman', said another, 'white of fur, affable with great and small'. A sculptor made a memorial effigy, a plaque was placed on the café wall, and Horatio Brown, the English historian of Venice, supposing that Nini spent his night hours roaming the Archives as Brown himself spent the day, ended a memorial apostrophe with the words:

> *What wit and learning died with you,*
> *What wisdom too!*
> *Take these poor verses, feline cat,*
> *Indited by an Archive rat.*

And a third feline celebrity, sad to tell, was made famous only by the manner of its death. On 14 July 1902, the great Campanile of San Marco, on the corner of the Piazza, subsided into a pile of rubble. This calamity was not unexpected. The tower had stood there since the tenth century, and was weakening year by year: repeatedly struck by lightning, injudiciously altered and enlarged, buffeted by so many sea-winds, rotted by so much salt air that by the beginning of the twentieth century it was ready to resign. The Venetian engineers recognized the fact, and a few days before its collapse prepared for the event. The midday gun was cancelled, in case it shook the old building, the Piazza bands were silenced, the custodian and his wife, who lived in the red loggia at the foot of the tower, evacuated their home with all their belongings and their tabby cat Mélampyge. The Piazza was roped off. The people sadly waited.

At five to ten that morning it happened. With a tremendous shudder the tower reluctantly collapsed, to a sigh that echoed around the nations. There were no human casualties. The golden angel from the tower's summit fell unhurt at the door of the Basilica, and the great bell called the Marangona was found unbroken amidst the debris. That same evening the city councillors resolved that the tower would be rebuilt *com'era, dov'era* – as it was, where it was.

Only the poor cat Mélampyge, returning that morning to the loggia unawares, was martyred by the fall.

* * *

From the common cat (*felis catus*), the Venetians, their horizons enlarged by their imperial and commercial adventures, turned to the lion (*leo leo*), and were eventually besotted by him. *Leo leo* turned their heads! They built him into their corbels, they slipped him into their allegories, they stuck him on gateposts, they made him the cornerstones of bridges. Citizens kept live lions in their gardens, and for a time a State Lion lived in a golden cage in the Piazza: he died, it is said, because licking the bars gave him gilt poisoning, and thereafter captive lions were forbidden in the city for several centuries. When one turned up, though, at the Venetian Carnival of 1762, Pietro Longhi showed him grandly on display, with a little dog on his back, dancing dogs all around him, a monkey on a beam above, a fiddler fiddling, and the strolling Venetians engrossed as ever by his presence.

St Jerome ranked high in the Venetian hagiography partly because he was a Dalmatian saint, and therefore a Venetian colonial, but partly perhaps because of his association with the lion. Most Venetian lion-pictures portray St Jerome's devoted companion (from whose paw he had removed a thorn), and wonderfully varied are their interpretations. Carlo Crivelli, painting in the fifteenth century, made the beast almost Celtically stylized, all long wavy mane and curled tongue. Lorenzo Lotto painted him rather ugly and very small, timidly peering from behind a tree-stump while the saint consults his sacred books. Carpaccio, in his sequence about St Jerome in the Scuola degli Schiavoni, paints him all winsome appeal – baffled and a little aggrieved, it seems, when his appearance sends the inhabitants of a monastery scattering panic-stricken in all directions, and just to be seen heart-broken in the background as the funeral rites are read over his old master's peaceful corpse.

But St Jerome's friend apart, every kind of lion is to be encountered in a stroll around Venice, on paintings, in sculptures, in bas-relief. There are lions in the middle of dreadful meals, lions having their jaws wrenched open, lions with crowns on their heads, lions confronted by dragons, the lion that carries Minerva side-saddle in the public gardens, the eighteenth-century red marble lions of the Piazzetta dei Leoncini which seem specifically designed to let children ride them, the benignly simpering Byzantine lions that sustain the Tree of Life in the cathedral screen at Torcello.

Best of all, there is the quartet of sculpted lions that stands outside the gates of the Arsenal, the centre of Venetian naval power until the fall of the Republic in 1797. They have strange stories to tell. One, looking a little like a mongoose, was looted from the island of Delos, where some of its companions remain. One was sent headless from Greece by Morosini, when he briefly re-conquered Athens for Venice in the seventeenth century: he had failed in his ambition to acquire for the Republic part of the frieze of the Parthenon, which his engineers had been unable to remove intact, so as a substitute he dispatched this ancient animal from the Sacred Way – 'you can easily get another head from somewhere', he told the

Signory, and so it evidently proved. And the tall gaunt lion on the left, towering above his colleagues and guarding the ceremonial doorway to the naval base, once stood at the entrance to the Piraeus, and indeed gave the harbour its ancient name of Lion's Port. In classical times water gushed out of this creature's mouth, and on its haunches, still faintly to be seen, is carved a runic inscription: it was chiselled there, it is thought, by Norse mercenaries in the employ of the Byzantine Emperor, long, long ago when Venice was only up-and-coming.

* * *

Leo leo has lost his majesty a little, now that he is to be seen so often, supine and flabby, in zoos and safari parks across the world, and for years nobody has erected a new leonine image in Venice. For the moment, though, his cousin the common cat, rules there still in urchin throng and conclave: and sometimes I think that if ever the worst happens, the rising waters flood the city at last and the Venetians withdraw once more to the mainland, sororities of cats will flourish still among the ruins, yawning, squabbling and sunning themselves in abandoned palaces, delicately extracting fish from flooded courtyards, and even perhaps, in their new autonomy, occasionally snatching a pigeon.

6 MISCELLANY OF MAMMALS

Hark! There sounds upon the Venetian air a strange cacophony of voices – neighs, bellows, grunts, yaps, squeaks, howls and belches. There were no mammals indigenous to the lagoon proper, when the Venetians moved into it, but mammals of many kinds have made their contribution to the Venetian achievement. Cats and dogs we know about: let us look now into less frequented corners of the menagerie, and see what beasts of truth or deception are making all that noise.

* * *

For many years the horse was truth. In the early centuries of settlement, when the bridges over the Venetian canals were all flat, horses were brought into the lagoon in their thousands. Nobody ever actually 'went through Venice in post', as a tall-story traveller claimed to old Coryat, but for the monied classes at least the normal way to get from one side of metropolitan Venice to the other was, as in all other cities of Europe, by riding a horse.

The aristocrats vied with each other then not only in the vivid fittings of their gondolas, but in the trappings of their horses too. When in 1362 the poet Petrarch was present at a jousting tournament in the Piazza, he admiringly declared the Venetians 'a nation of horsemen', and in the fifteenth century the exhibitionist Doge Michel Steno maintained a stable of four hundred horses, their coats all dyed yellow, which was claimed to be the finest in Europe. In those days the Grand Council of the Republic assembled for their meetings at the Doge's Palace on horseback, and the bell in the Campanile called the Trottiera rang, so it said, when they needed to hurry. (There were mules and donkeys about, too, but these were mostly ridden by women and ecclesiastics, who were perhaps better able to manage them.)

Frightful stinks and hazards must have been caused by so many horses in such a city, and very early in their history the Venetians laid down laws for the restriction of horseback traffic. By the fourteenth century horses were compelled to wear warning bells, and they were forbidden to enter the Piazza: those coming from the Rialto were tethered to the clump of elder trees then growing at the Piazza end of the Mercerie, while on the eastern side the Ponte de Paglia, the Bridge of Straw, is said to have been the place where the animals were left with their feeding-bags. Then a toll was levied on horsemen going to Rialto by way of San Salvador, to prevent congestion, and eventually horses were banned altogether from the Mercerie, which thus became an early prototype of today's pedestrian shopping precincts. (The last man ever to ride down it, we are told, was a convicted procurer, who was led between the shops on a donkey, dressed all in yellow and bearing a pair of horns upon his head.)

The equestrian display of Venice was tempered rather when the sixteenth-century sumptuary laws, which restrained ostentation in private gondolas, were applied to horses' gear too, and as humped bridges appeared throughout the city, allowing bigger boats to pass beneath, so the horse gradually withdrew from the canal-side streets. 'I saw but one horse in all Venice', reported Coryat in 1611; by 1789 Dr Johnson's friend Mrs Thrale was recording a queue to see a stuffed horse in a sideshow. Later a few animals were imported for hacking in the public gardens and on the island called the Lido, and during the Austrian occupation, in the first half of the nineteenth century, cavalry were garrisoned by the docks, their horses being exercised in a Champs de Mars near the water's edge. As a means of transport, though, the Venetian horse was dead by then, and foreigners who came to Venice with their own horses were obliged to stable them at great expense on the mainland: John Ruskin, commenting upon a figure of Folly, on a Doge's Palace capital, which consisted simply of a horseback figure, suggested dryly that it was 'worth the consideration of the English residents who bring their horses to Venice'.

Still, if the live horses have gone, the pavements of Venice are enlivened by some striking sculpted ones. There is the terrific equestrian figure of the condottiere Bartolomeo Colleoni, the last work of the sculptor Andrea Verrocchio, which was erected in 1489 outside the church of SS Giovanni e Paolo. This colossal piece, all snort and swagger from man and beast alike, used to be gilded: Carpaccio included a fanciful version of it in the background of his picture of St Stephen, looking if anything even more magnificent than the original, and I like to think that Giovanni Bellini, who must have seen the statue go up, orientalized it in the strutting Arab, ridden by a gloriously turbaned bravo of the East, who appears in the background of his *Madonna and Child* now at Bergamo.

Then there is the fine and florid horse, the only Romantic horse in Venice, which carries the effigy of King Vittorio Emanuele II on the Riva degli Schiavoni – designed by the Roman sculptor Ettore Ferrari, erected in 1887, and surrounded all about, as in a heaving of bronze, by lions couchant and emblematic enthusiasms. Finally in our own time the American collector Peggy Guggenheim embellished the Grand Canal itself by placing an equestrian figure in the courtyard of her Palazzo Venier dei Leoni, directly beside the water. Created by the Milanese Marino Marini, who was born in 1901, this, though thin, is the lustiest of the Venetian horses, for both beast and rider are in a condition of perpetual sexual ecstasy –

as though the glorious panorama before their eyes, or the very seduction of Venice all around, has inflamed the two of them for ever.

There are water-horses, too, for the memory of the living horse survives in the black shapes of the gondolas, with their horse-heads of steel at the prow: when they are moored they look like restive hunters in their stalls, all high-strung pent-up elegance, and when they are out on the lagoon they leap, and toss, and bound over the waves like thoroughbreds.

*   *   *

It cannot have been long, when once the Venetian settlements were established, before the first herdsmen brought cattle to the islands, the shepherds a few sheep for mutton, the pigmen their sows and boars – indeed until 1409, when they were banned, monastery pigs used to run all over the city, protected by law and fed by pious householders. One old legend associates both sheep and cows with the foundation of San Pietro di Castello, the original metropolitan cathedral of Venice, in the eighth century or thereabouts: St Peter, it is said, appeared personally before the Bishop of Heraclia, another migratory prelate from the mainland, and commanded him to build a church in his honour 'where there should be seen oxen and sheep grazing together'. ('What there was so prodigious in oxen and sheep feeding together', Ruskin remarks in *The Stones of Venice*, 'we need St Peter, I think, to tell us: but the prodigy lay, perhaps, in their grazing there at all.')

Until Venice was connected to the mainland by a causeway, in 1846, many dairies flourished in the city, served often by a couple of cows in a backyard shed. In the nineteenth century the English community kept its own herd, distrusting the hygiene no doubt of anyone else's, and in our own day the Franciscan monks on the island of San Francesco del Deserto, whose guardian cypresses you may see away in the northern expanses of the lagoon, have always kept a couple of milking cows in a barn, along with ducks, hens and peacocks.

I have never heard of cattle-breeding in the Venetian archipelago, but there was a time when bulls were familiar enough in the city, because the sport of bull-baiting was popular there until the beginning of the nineteenth century, when it was prohibited by the French occupation authorities. In the Piazza and several of the neighbourhood squares men, boys and dogs pitted themselves against tethered bulls, the most popular arena of all being the Campo San Polo on the north side of the Grand Canal. Joseph Heintz the Younger pictured a tournament there in 1648, and a hectic afternoon it seems to have been. The bulls are scattered in separate contests over the square, and all around them frenzy reigns – dogs barking everywhere, men flat on the ground or crawling to safety, bulls lunging here and there, and only a few grand ladies with their children sauntering disdainfully in satin fineries past the commotion.

Sheep were always herded, of course, in the salt-water meadows that fringe the lagoon, and some were kept on the big green islands of Sant'Erasmo and Vignole, traditionally the farmlands of the city. Flocks safely graze in the backgrounds of many a Venetian painting, and most hauntingly perhaps in the lyric landscapes of Giorgione, himself a native of Castelfranco on the nearby mainland – sheep preter-naturally still in their hilly pastures, watched over by tranced shepherds in the enigmatic suspension of time that Giorgione pre-eminently conjured. The prize Venetian sheep, though, is not at large in any meadow, and occupies not the background, but the very front, of a great painting. In Lorenzo Lotto's *Madonna* in the church of Santo Spirito at Bergamo, the Virgin Mary sits with her baby upon an elevated throne, orientally carpeted, while a host of angels serenades her with lutes and trumpets in the sky, and various saints stand in attendance.

At the foot of the throne a naked cherub, holding a cross in his right hand, at the same time violently clutches a lamb. Every parent will recognize the relationship between the two. The cherub is almost strangling the little creature with the strength of his affection: the lamb, knocked skew-whiff by the embrace, one ear up, one down, looks out at us with an expression of throttled long-suffering, concentrating particularly, one supposes, on continuing to breathe.

*   *   *

Less domesticated mammals of town and country made themselves known to the Venetians, too. Foxes certainly live on the mainland shores of the lagoon, and may well, at one time or another, somehow have migrated to the islands. They long ago found lairs in Venetian art, anyway, no doubt because their irrepressible cleverness, their eye for the main chance, struck a chord among the not altogether *un*-foxy Venetians; but as it happens the most familiar Venetian fox is depicted in a moment of humiliation.

This is the unhappy fellow depicted in the twelfth-century mosaic floor of the basilica of SS Maria e Donato at Murano, one of the chief Byzantine monuments of the lagoon. The scene allegorically represents Watchfulness triumphing over Cunning, and it shows two insufferably self-satisfied cocks carrying on a pole between them the body of their hereditary enemy. I am not sure if the fox is dead or alive: the surface of the floor, consisting as it does of such venerable chips, undulates rather, and this gives the design a curious sense of animation, as in an early Disney cartoon, and makes one feel that in the mind of the artist at least, if not in the intention of his pious clients, Cunning might not be defeated after all, and Master Reynard might yet wriggle off that pole and away down the nave into the sunshine.

Rabbits breed contentedly on the deserted island of Poveglia, in the southern lagoon, a pair having been settled there in 1945 to provide meals for its now defunct old people's home. As for the verminous smaller mammals, they have doubtless been in the lagoon almost as long as the humans, and proliferate always among the attics, the skirting-boards and the mud. The rats you hardly ever see. You may catch sight of one slinking greedily among the empty stalls of the market after dark; more often they reveal themselves only in death, swirling with protruding belly and waterlogged tail down the Grand Canal towards the merciful sea. The mice are more visible, and are everywhere: under church seats, behind refrigerators, beneath monumental Renaissance staircases. Down all the ages of Venetian history they have remained inexpungable, and twice at least, the official records of the Basilica show, with their insatiable nibblings they have silenced the mighty organ of San Marco.

* * *

More exotic animal images, and for that matter more exotic animals, were brought home by the Venetians from their wanderings. The very nature of the city depended upon its ancient connections with Asia and North Africa. Turbaned Moors figured largely in its art and annals, loot from Byzantium and the Levant ornamented its churches and stocked its ample treasuries. Inevitably creatures from distant parts entered the civic imagination too.

The most obvious candidate for naturalization was the camel, the very symbol of that Muslim world upon which Venetian prosperity so largely depended, and sure enough he appears here and there in sculpture, and very often of course in scenes of Biblical events or Christian allegory. If he is cautiously delineated as a rule, it is probably because the painters, in the absence of a living model, were not at all sure about the details of his anatomy, especially his hump. The camel in Tintoretto's *Abduction of the Body of St Mark* hardly seems to have a hump at all; Jacopo Bassano, when he painted a camel queuing to enter the Ark, prudently covered his hump with a concealing cloth; the hump of the thirteenth-century relief of a camel that gives its name to the Palazzo del Camello, near the church of Madonna dell'Orto, is handily obliterated by a load of merchandise. Anyway, there was something about the animal that did not suit the Venetian style. So ungainly, so discomfiting, he was the exact opposite of the snuggly, svelte or stately creatures they most loved. Their *chiaroscuro* could do little with the camel's dun desert colouring, their splendour of line could do nothing with that silhouette, and on the whole the camel was one of the less successful creatures of the Venetian bestiary.

You might think the most inept to be the specimens

on the façade of the church of San Moise, which was decorated by Arrigo Meyring in the late seventeenth century, for they are preposterously disjointed and contorted of posture; but actually worse examples still sustain the funerary trophies of the Doge Giovanni Pesaro in the Frari church, thought to have been designed, in the 1660s, by Baldassare Longhena. Some people deny that these are camels at all, but they are meant to be, I think, the Pesaro clan having distinguished itself in the East. They are cameloid in an unnerving way, however. They have necks like tortoises and heads like iguanas, their entire forms seem somehow blotched and spasmed, as though they have been visited by some dread Arabian pest, and among all the beasts of Venice they must be accounted, I am afraid, quite the nastiest.

There is no record of a camel visiting Venice in the flesh, but from time to time other surprising exotics have turned up in the city. In the nineteenth century a monkey lived for many years on the island of San Servolo, the municipal lunatic asylum for men, and was often to be seen sunning himself among the poor patients in the garden. In the twentieth century a grandee home from conquered Ethiopia brought a cheetah with him, and used to display it glamorously, like a Persian general home from Babylon, in his gondola on the Grand Canal.

The first elephant to show himself in the lagoon is said to have been shipped there by the Sultan of Turkey, to be taken over the Alps to Vienna as a present for the Hapsburg court, but many successors have disembarked in Venice since, and you may still see one sometimes when a circus comes to town. Pietro Longhi shows us an elephant who arrived in 1774: not a very large one, he is heavily shackled upon a platform, observed by three masked gentlefolk, and in the background the artist himself is to be seen making his preliminary sketches – as it says in a large inscription immediately above his head, the picture is a TRUE PORTRAIT OF THE ELEPHANT BROUGHT TO VENICE IN THE YEAR 1774.

Longhi painted a rhinoceros once, too, and this unfortunate beast may provide a properly poignant conclusion to our miscellany of mammals (for there is something a little wistful about the translation of these animals to so alien a setting). In 1751, when this beast arrived in Europe, hardly anyone had ever seen a rhinoceros – probably none had come to the continent since the specimen made famous by Dürer's etching of 1515. The creature had made a triumphal tour of the capitals, being measured, weighed and lectured about everywhere, and in Venice Longhi was commissioned by one of the great patricians of the day, Giovanni Grimani, to paint a formal portrait. It is a sad little scene. Longhi's usual knot of Venetians, some masked, inspects the animal without noticeable excitement, and the rhinoceros itself, looking pig-like, stands lethargic in his pit gazing into nowhere and listlessly chewing straw. The only sign of vivacity is provided by a boy, perhaps the keeper, who seems about to whack the animal on his scaly back with his raised whip. The rhinoceros takes no notice. Chew, chew, he stands there, plonk on his four flat feet, dreaming of Africa.

7 FANTASY OF MONSTERS

Behind the high altar of the basilica at Murano, in the dim light of the apse, not far from that distressful fox, you may discern a curious clutter of objects upon the wall. They are rather hard to see. Greyish in colour, spindly in form, they might be ancient weapons, or ivory votive offerings. In fact, or at least in fantasy, they are the bones of a dragon.

St Donato, one of the saints to whom the church is dedicated, miraculously slew a dragon on the Greek island of Cephalonia simply by spitting at it. His body was brought to Venice as a sacred relic, by Crusaders returning from the east, and with it there came, in a separate container, the bones of the beast he slew. They are the only anatomical exhibits, I think, but they are certainly not the only examples of this city's preoccupation with mythical or mutated beasts. Neither quite fish nor altogether fowl, mammalian in some respects, reptilian in others, in Venice there be monsters.

*   *   *

The Venetian view of the natural world is generally benign, but the image of its unnatural inhabitants, perhaps to point a contrast, is often more disturbing. Especially in sculpture there are some unlovely chimerae about, like the half-human, half-animal creature on the wall of the church of Santa Maria Formosa, bulging its eyes and licking its lips, which the fastidious Ruskin thought 'too foul to be either pictured or described, or to be beheld for more than an instant'.

The city crawls with freaks and hybrids – on the Doge's Palace alone you may find the human form half-mutated into serpent, horse, fish and bear – and there are stone dragons and griffins all over the place. Two fight each other agonizingly to the death on the wall of the church of Santa Margherita, now a cinema; on the south face of the Basilica a macabre pair crouch at their victuals, one grasping a supine ox while the other, holding a distraught maiden between his claws, appears to be saying grace. It comes as no surprise to find that, while the figure of Obedience on the Doge's Palace is attended by a charmingly begging dog, the neighbouring effigy of Envy not only has snakes wreathed about her head and waist, but also cherishes, nestling malevolently in her lap as if it might be a kitten or a Pekingese, a small but horrid dragon.

On the other hand in Venetian painting your average monster is more prepossessing. He often turns out to be surprisingly small, and is inclined to look less dragon-like than weaselly. Though his role is nearly

always villainous, sometimes he even excites a certain
sympathy in us, as the fatal lance is thrust into his
smoky snout, and the assembled chivalry applauds
the end of him. Jacopo Bellini, in one of those innumerable Venetian celebrations of St Jerome, gives us
a positively fawning monster of the wilderness, spine-
backed but curiously elfin, and gazing appeasingly
into the eyes of the holy man as he kneels at prayer.
His son Giovanni Bellini imagines some unalarm-
ing centaurs. The dragons of Tintoretto would surely
wring a tear from St Donato himself: for if one coura-
geously resists the onslaught of St George on the very
edge of an ocean, clinging to the shore for dear life
itself, another, already speared through the brain, is
being sat upon by his intended victim the princess,
and looks out from beneath her ample form like a
lobster from a pot.

Carpaccio seems temperamentally incapable of pre-
senting an *entirely* horrible monster. It is true that the
dragon he invented for the fulfilment of St George in
the Scuola degli Schiavoni is surrounded by the mangled limbs and foreshortened chewed torsos of late
victims and earlier opponents, but the creature himself, who has a dog's head, a lion's legs, a serpent's
tail, big clawed forefeet and scaly wings, is really
rather graceful. Near by Carpaccio has painted a
scene showing the infant St Tryphone, a Dalmatian
martyr, exorcising a demon out of an emperor's
daughter. Here was a chance for some truly mon-
strous portraiture, since the demon had taken the

form of a basilisk, who was born out of an egg laid by a cock and hatched by a serpent, and whose very glare could kill a man. But no: Carpaccio's quaint cockatrice struts away from the imperial presence with an expression not of evil or even malice, but only of infinitely comical reproach, and looks less like a manifestation of Satan than a large, prickly and cocky sort of earwig.

* * *

And if you count a unicorn as a monster, then the delicate Venetian unicorn in Giorgione's *Chastity* must surely be the loveliest chimera, the most trustful, the most comforting, altogether the best, ever to lay its white horned head upon a maiden's knee.

8 TEAM OF CHAMPIONS

Ah, but I have left the mightiest till last! More wonderful than all these beasts, far older than most of them, ever present in the city of Venice are five prodigies of the animal kingdom: four Golden Stallions, by war out of mystery, one Winged Lion, by power out of faith. No city ever had such allies among the creatures, and no bestiary was ever headed by such a noble team of champions.

* * *

For nearly six hundred years the Golden Stallions of St Mark were the pride and comfort of the Venetian Republic. They were miraculous stallions. They first came prancing into history (for their stance was sprightly) in the year 1204, when the Fourth Crusade, shipped and mostly directed by the Venetians, captured Constantinople and demolished the Byzantine Empire.

Somewhere in the sacked city the Venetians found the four horses – on the imperial pavilion at the

Hippodrome, perhaps, or beside the gates of the
Great Palace, the very centre of Byzantine power.
Of the horses' provenance we know nothing certain.
Perhaps they were Roman work – the half-moon
structure of their eyes, some theorists maintain, was
specifically a Roman device. Perhaps they were
much, much older, and were conceived by some
refulgent genius of classical Greece. Larger than
life-size, they once pulled a chariot, and they looked
to be horses of stout working stock – yeomen horses,
as it were. Their hides of gold covered a primitive
alloy, hardly fit to be called bronze, but there was
nothing crude to their conception. So subtle, elegant
and powerful were their forms, so true to life and
yet so full of suggestion, that like all great works of
art they generated a magnetism far beyond their
substance.

The Venetians, anyway, recognized their divine
quality from the start, and so the Golden Horses came
to the lagoon (slightly damaged in transit – one hoof
was broken off, and stood for years above the doorway of the ship's captain). They were the ultimate
loot, and they were placed on the ultimate exhibition
shelf, above the doorway of the Basilica San Marco,
looking out across the Piazza. It is probable that when
they hauled their chariot the outer two horses tossed
their heads outwards, the central two inwards. The
Venetians mounted them instead in separated pairs,
each pair of animals inclining their heads towards
each other, and this perhaps gave them a gentler look,

less tempestuous but more compassionate, like four friends.

Beloved friends they became indeed to the citizens of Venice, and symbols to every foreigner of the Republic's unshakeable fortitude. They were the most reassuring of all the devices that gave such all-confident splendour to the city, the very eponyms of La Serenissima, The Most Serene, as the Republic liked to call itself, and they seemed to have been there always. In the one surviving thirteenth-century mosaic above the Basilica doors they are seen clearly *in situ*; in that earliest of Venetian view-pictures, from *The Book of Marco Polo*, they stand like enamelled toys among the fanciful turrets and swan-swum waterways; and until the fall of Venice scarcely a painter in the place failed to portray them, sometimes directly, sometimes by allusion. Not only were they the most accessible models of horseflesh in the city, they had become part of every Venetian's aesthetic equipment.

Tintoretto included one of them, as a centurion's charger, in his monumental *Crucifixion* in the Scuola San Rocco, while Lotto places all four at the foot of the Cross, and one more, in haunting and shadowy silhouette, at the bottom of Pontius Pilate's staircase. From the saddle of a Golden Stallion Carpaccio's St Martin leans down to greet his beggar, and Carpaccio also puts a model of one on St Augustine's study mantelpiece. Jacopo Bassano turned two of them into unicorns for the stocking of the Ark;

Canaletto, in a famous caprice, removed them all from the Basilica and mounted them on four separate pedestals in the Piazzetta. In Gentile Bellini's picture *The Procession of the True Cross through the Piazza*, painted in 1496, the horses are not only to be seen shining celestially on their gallery, but, as in a Russian toy, are also there in minuscule reduction in the mosaic above the door.

During the centuries, between the Romans and the Renaissance, when the art of equestrian sculpture was lost to Europe, the Golden Horses must have seemed like visitors from Heaven itself, and indeed they became the almost supernatural guarantors of Venetian stability, framed as they so often were by the billowing flags on the great bronze flagstaffs that stood in the Piazza before them. So long as they stood up there, it was thought, the Republic would retain its liberty, its wealth and its command of the sea. When in 1379 the Genoese admiral Pietro Doria was poised at the very sea-gate of Venice, ready to humiliate the Serenissima at last, he boasted that there would be 'no peace until we have curbed your unbridled horses'. He spoke too rashly. Within the year he was dead, all his ships and men had ignominiously surrendered, and the power of Genoa was permanently broken.

Nobody bridled the Golden Horses until Napoleon's forces, seizing the city in 1797, shipped them away to Paris with the rest of the booty. They returned after Napoleon's fall, but their spell was never quite the same again: Venice never regained her independence, and like everything else in the city the horses acquired a new sort of suggestiveness, a hint of melancholy, a trace of resignation. They were removed from their galleries again, for safety's sake, during each of the world wars, and now at last they have gone for ever from their lofty stable, to be preserved as charms or talismans no longer, but only as museum pieces. You may see them through the doors of their last resting place, inside the Basilica, still in their old magnanimous postures, their forehoofs raised, their heads tilted in comradeship; but on their belvedere outside, where they defied the climate and proclaimed the spirit of Venice for so many centuries, only bland and lifeless replicas remain.

The Venetians mourned their going, as they grieved in the past whenever the divine animals were removed from their façade. The saddest Venetian pictures I know are photographs of the Golden Stallions being removed from the Basilica during the First World War. It seems to have been a grey winter day. The workmen are muffled in thick greatcoats, the bystanders are huddled against the chill, and as the four lovely figures are lowered by pulleys from their plinths and taken silently away, looking proudly this way and that – as they disappear into the grey it is as though some sun gods are withdrawing, mythic messengers from brighter times and holier places, taking the light with them.

* * *

The Golden Stallions championed the liberty of Venice: a monster, but a monster of heroic splendour exerted the Republic's far-flung authority.

In the ninth century two Venetian merchants smuggled out of Islamic Egypt the body of St Mark, and brought it reverently and triumphantly to Venice. The Evangelist replaced St Theodore as patron saint of the Republic, and a convenient body of legend arose to connect him more intimately and anciently with the lagoon. Around his remains was built the tremendous Basilica; around his name grew up the power and reputation of the Republic.

And with St Mark, into the sensibility of the Venetians there entered the first of the Four Beasts in the Book of Revelation, who had long since become, at the recommendation of St Jerome actually, the Evangelist's symbol and companion. In the Bible he was full of eyes before, behind and within, and he had six wings about him. In Venice he was simplified, and converted from a mystical vision into a National Beast. Out went the crocodile of St Theodore, to survive only upon his Piazzetta pillar. In came the Winged Lion of St Mark, and he went on guard wherever the Venetians ruled, from the islands of the lagoon itself to remote castles of Crete and Cyprus, to Naxos or Nauplia in the Aegean, to Corfu, Cephalonia and the old sea-cities of the Yugoslav coast.

The winged lion is a propagandist's dream. Since his first appearance on the Venetian flag, probably in the thirteenth century, he has been essential to

86

the Venetian swagger. Sometimes he holds a sword, sometimes a flag, occasionally the Doge's ceremonial flag, and there is almost always a book, presumably St Mark's gospel, in, between, or under his front paws. On its pages are generally inscribed words alleged to have been spoken to St Mark by an angel during an otherwise undocumented visit to the lagoon some four centuries before the foundation of Venice – PAX TIBI MARCE EVANGELISTA MEUS, Peace Unto Thee Mark My Evangelist – but sometimes this volume is closed, to express a leonine displeasure, or blank, or in foreign parts inscribed with more threatening texts, like Let God Arise And Let His Enemies Be Scattered.

Venetian designers, down the ages, so exploited the physique of the winged lion (skilfully blurring, more often than not, the awkward anatomical junction, under the wings, where fur must give way to feather) that at one time or another he has satisfied every kind of aesthetic requirement and completed all manner of architectural ensemble. He has been squashed and distended and elongated and truncated, or bunched into squareness to fit an alcove or a coin (in which form he used to be called the *moleca*, because he reminded the Venetians of a particular sort of crab). Carpaccio, in the best known of all his representations, gives him grinning teeth and a slightly Lancashire look. Tintoretto, in his enormous *Paradise* in the Doge's Palace, has him cuddled up beside his master like a favoured pet – discussing with the Evangelist,

Mark Twain once suggested, the correct spelling of a word. The huge winged lion above the gate of the Arsenal holds the Gospel open in his paws – but it bears no text. The pug-like winged lion on the column in the Piazzetta, alongside St Theodore, began life not as a lion at all, but as a Levantine, Persian, or even perhaps Chinese chimera: his book was inserted under his paws when he was brought to Venice from the east, and his agate eyes have eyelashes.

But then he is innumerable. There are winged prides of him in Venice. He was stamped, engraved, embroidered or carved upon every official document, coin, banner òr entablature, and he stands magnificently still in every position of power: above the main doorway of the Basilica, above the main entrance to the Doge's Palace, above the gateway of the Arsenal, high on the Campanile San Marco, beneath the great bell of the Clock Tower, on the tops of the three bronze flagstaffs. Napoleon ordered the extinction of the winged lion, and a scoundrelly Venetian mason actually signed a contract with the French for the defacement or removal of every specimen in the city. He never honoured the agreement, however, most of the images were left intact, and though many generations have passed now since Venice lost her imperial authority, still to this day the Winged Lion is vigorously alive.

He strides to sea on the funnels of ships. He travels the world on souvenir paperweights. He is imprinted on carrier-bags, moulded into door-knockers, stuck on walls as insurance plates. He is the undisputed boss of the bestiary. Wherever you see him now, in whatever circumstances, you think first not of the saintly Evangelist, still less of those other, all-eyed chanting Beasts around the mystic throne, but first and always of Venice.

9 THE COMPANIONSHIP

Many nations have found it necessary in some way to identify with the world of the animals, and to adopt some creature real or mythical as their particular consort through history – the American eagle, the French cock, the Russian bear, the British lion, the wolf of Rome or the dragon of Wales. Sometimes they adopted a beast-emblem out of feudal custom, or the necessities of battle: sometimes they saw in their chosen creature the qualities they coveted for themselves, like majesty, daring or ferocity (for they seldom picked animals of symbolic modesty, the loyal pelican, the lamb or the chaste unicorn . . . .)

The Venetians went further than most, and made a brotherhood of their bestiary. The winged lion was more than just a formal figurehead, but a delegate of the Republic; the Golden Horses were beloved with a true passion; and if there is a single impression to be gained from all the thousands of Venetian animal images, it is one of wry and comradely fondness. In Venetian art the pet frequently looks more prepossessing than its master, just as in Venetian life, today as always, the animal sometimes gets gentler treatment than the man. The animal legends of Venice are seldom legends of hostility: sea-birds are helpful, cats are loyal, lions lie affectionately at the feet of saints, pigeons bring news of victory, cows and sheep give guidance to ecclesiastical surveyors and even monsters seem to bear no grudge. It is said that in Roman times the people of the Veneto disliked gladiatorial contests with wild beasts, preferring chariot races every time, and there is no compromise, among the works of the Venetian masters, with cruelty towards the beasts – the duck-hunt is made to look ridiculous, and the worst of the dragons dies in fair fight.

No doubt the loneliness of their circumstances made the Venetians more than usually tender towards their fellow creatures, and gave the birds, beasts and fishes such prominence in their art. Foreigners in Venice, after all, have seldom been preoccupied with animal subjects. It is true that Dürer's famous crab was a Venetian specimen, painted during a visit in the 1490s, but animals seldom show in foreign view-paintings of the city – there is not a cat beside Corot's Grand Canal, not a night-bird above Whistler's lagoon, not a single gull circling around Monet's luminous Doge's Palace or a dog in Dufy's *campi*. But the Venetians themselves saw animals everywhere – and not least in those very pastoral settings, of lush meadows and hospitable hills, which their civic circumstances denied them. They were longing, I suppose, for a softer greenness in their lives, for the slow comforting movement of the sheep on the hillside, the stir of cattle in the byre.

And as a nation they yearned too, perhaps, for innocent companionship, if only in the imagination. For much of their history they were a people uncomfortably on their own. Physically they were more lonely than other city dwellers; politically they were respected, admired, feared but seldom loved. If they were at war with the Muslims for centuries at a time, to Christian Europe they often seemed like traitors. Their gaudy half-oriental tastes, their ornery kind of Catholicism, their reputation for intrigue and mayhem, all isolated them among the Powers; and anyway they liked to think of themselves, at least in their early years, as the only true descendants of the Romans, and thus in a class apart.

Perhaps it is no wonder, then, that they cherished the idea of the animals. Kenneth Clark tells us that during the glory years of the High Renaissance man forgot his kinship with the beasts – 'it was only in Venice that art retained its necessary warmth . . .' That warmth sustained the Venetian bestiary always. I have identified only a few of its members in this monograph, but there is really hardly a creature of the Creation, or beyond it come to that, which does not appear somewhere or other in Venetian life or art. The idlest meander through the city's streets, the most casual impression of its pictures, is enough to demonstrate the virtuoso profusion of Venetian animal imagery. The Doge's Palace columns alone offer us snake, dolphin, bee, scorpion, dog, lion of course, lamb, cock, bear, bull, crab, wolf and monkey, not to speak of assorted monsters and innumerable birds. The mosaics of the Basilica are a nature reserve of their own, and you could spend a happy week in the Accademia art gallery just looking at the animals.

But perhaps in the end, when one thinks of the beasts of Venice, it is the living creatures that speak most vividly of the character of the place, remind us most pungently of its harsh beginnings, and best suggest to us the marvellous continuity of its history. The Stallions are humiliated, within their shadowy museum. Staunchly though Colleoni's great charger still stands upon his pedestal, he has lost a little of his force now that so few of us know the name of his rider. Even the winged lion is deprived of sovereignty: though he survives sinewy or over-weight, reproving or amiable, from one end of Venice to the other, and far beyond to the very ends of the Mediterranean, still his imperial pretensions are all hollow, and nobody cares two hoots whether his book is closed or open.

But the *real* animals of Venice take us back to the origins of the place. They have changed far less than the people. The same myriad crabs sidle around the waterlines of Venice now as sidled around the first wattle-huts of the refugees. The cats who skulk beneath those bridges skulked, I do not doubt, in the original market-places of Rivo Alto, and foraged then as now among the bones and innards left for them by sentimental well-wishers. That dog has been standing at the prow of his barge since the Middle Ages: Carpaccio's little terrier long preceded the artist, and has merrily survived him.

It is the sea-birds of the lagoon, though, that we must honour still as the presiding spirits of the city. The lagoon was the beginning of Venice, and may one day be its end, and over it now, as then, as ever will be, the sea-birds squawk, swoop and flutter, bobbing on glistening ripples in the sunshine, flocking after ships to the open sea, messing about on mud-banks when the tide is low, morosely meditating on mooring-posts. I love these brave survivors! I love their restless flight over the waste waters, and their truculent poses on the heads of statues. I love the rude vitality of them, when they skirmish over fish-ends or dispute the droppings of garbage-boats. And most of all they move me when, in the middle of the night, they are to be seen dimly wavering here and there in the lamplight of the quays.

The city sleeps then. Only a solitary midnight boat labours across the Bacino, perhaps, and there is a clanging of hulls and chains among the off-duty water-buses moored along the Riva. But out there above the black water, sweeping in and out of the light, the Venetian sea-birds, now as always, fly erratically through the small hours. Sometimes they whirl out of sight into the upper darkness, sometimes they seem to stagger in their own slip-streams, and sometimes they sweep abruptly down to the surface of the lagoon, as if they are looking for something: squids I dare say, insects of the dark, or timeless essences that we know nothing of.

HISTORICAL SUMMARY

The Venetians, having moved into the lagoon sporadically during the fifth and sixth centuries, presently established themselves as an independent Republic, and elected their first Doge (or Duke) probably in 727. They became a great maritime and commercial power, specializing in the oriental trade, and by their part in the Fourth Crusade of 1202 acquired a profitable colonial empire in the eastern Mediterranean. At the same time, despite frequent embroilments in European wars and disputes, they evolved a remarkably stable system of aristocratic government, and produced an astonishing succession of great artists. By the end of the fifteenth century they stood at an apogee of wealth and prestige.

The growing and hostile power of Islam, the rise of new commercial rivals in Europe and the discovery of new routes to the eastern markets all contributed to the long decline of the Republic. Though the artistic genius of the place triumphantly survived, the overseas empire was gradually lost, commercial and maritime supremacy was conceded, and by the middle of the eighteenth century Venice was in a condition of stylish but enervated abasement. Napoleon seized the city in 1797, but in October of the same year it was ceded to Austria by the peace of Campo Formio, and in 1866 became part of the new Italian kingdom. Administratively united now with industrial suburbs on the mainland, contemporary Venice is a regional capital, an important port, a cultural centre and Europe's supreme tourist destination.